FREEDOM'S PROMISE

JAPANESE AMERICAN IMPRISONMENT

DURING WORLD WAR II

BY DUCHESS HARRIS, JD, PHD
WITH MARNE VENTURA

Cover image: In 1942 the US government ordered more than 100,000 Japanese Americans to leave their homes.

Core Library
An Imprint of Abdo Publishing
abdobooks.com

abdobooks.com

Published by Abdo Publishing, a division of ABDO, PO Box 398166, Minneapolis, Minnesota 55439.

Printed in the United States of America, North Mankato, Minnesota
092019
012020

THIS BOOK CONTAINS RECYCLED MATERIALS

Cover Photo: Dorothea Lange/Department of the Interior. War Relocation Authority/US National Archives and Records Administration

Interior Photos: Dorothea Lange/Department of the Interior. War Relocation Authority/US National Archives and Records Administration, 1, 6–7, 15, 20–21, 22; Eliot Elisofon/The LIFE Picture Collection/Getty Images, 5, 43; Red Line Editorial, 10, 29; Bettmann/Getty Images, 12–13; AP Images, 16; Clem Albers/Department of the Interior. War Relocation Authority/US National Archives and Records Administration, 26–27; Ansel Adams/Manzanar War Relocation Center photographs/Library of Congress, 31, 34–35; Jim Ruymen/UPI Photo Service/Newscom, 37; Paul Kitagaki Jr./Zuma Press/Newscom, 38

Editor: Maddie Spalding
Series Designer: Ryan Gale

Library of Congress Control Number: 2019942000

Publisher's Cataloging-in-Publication Data

Names: Harris, Duchess, author. | Ventura, Marne, author.
Title: Japanese American imprisonment during World War II / by Duchess Harris and Marne Ventura
Description: Minneapolis, Minnesota : Abdo Publishing, 2020 | Series: Freedom's promise | Includes online resources and index.
Identifiers: ISBN 9781532190841 (lib. bdg.) | ISBN 9781532176692 (ebook)
Subjects: LCSH: Japanese Americans--Evacuation and relocation, 1942-1945--Juvenile literature. | Internment camps--Juvenile literature. | World War, 1939-1945--Japanese Americans--Juvenile literature. | Race relations--Juvenile literature. | Japanese Americans--Civil rights--Juvenile literature. | Race discrimination--Juvenile literature.
Classification: DDC 940.53170--dc23

CONTENTS

A LETTER FROM DUCHESS

The imprisonment of Japanese Americans seems like it happened a long time ago, but some people who went through this experience are still alive. I was fortunate enough to hear George Takei speak. His story changed my outlook on this narrative.

Many people know George Takei as an actor on the TV show *Star Trek*. However, he lived a fascinating life before he became a TV star. Mr. Takei and his parents were Japanese Americans. They were forced to leave their home in California to live in a camp in Arkansas. America was fighting Japan in World War II. The US government felt threatened, so it detained Japanese Americans in prison camps.

Mr. Takei was a small child when he was imprisoned. When his family was later released, their home had been sold. They could only afford to live in a poor neighborhood. The Takei family was able to rebuild their life. But not all Japanese Americans who were imprisoned were as fortunate. Please join me on a journey that questions the promise of freedom for Japanese Americans in the 1940s.

Duchess Harris

A group of Japanese Americans arrives at Manzanar prison camp in Owens Valley, California, in 1942.

CHAPTER ONE

LEAVING HOME

Something was wrong. Mary Matsuda and her brother had just gotten back from Sunday school. Her parents were sitting at the kitchen table. They looked worried. It was December 7, 1941. Mary was 17 years old. The Matsudas lived on Vashon Island in Washington State. Mary had grown up there. It was a lush, green town near Seattle. Her parents were Japanese immigrants. They had moved to the United States years ago from Japan. They were strawberry farmers.

Mary's father explained that Japan had bombed US ships in Pearl Harbor, Hawaii. Pearl Harbor was a US naval base. At the time, Japan was fighting in World War II (1939–1945).

In the 1940s, many Japanese Americans were farmers who lived in rural areas.

In response to the attack, the United States declared war on Japan.

Mary's parents feared the US government might treat them as enemies because they were Japanese American. The family gathered the belongings they had brought from Japan. They burned family photos, records, and books. They thought having things from Japan might make them appear loyal to Japan.

RELOCATION

In May 1942, the US government posted signs on telephone poles on Vashon Island. The signs said that all people of Japanese descent needed to be ready to leave within a few days. Each person could bring two suitcases.

On the day of the relocation, armed soldiers ordered people into US Army trucks. The trucks brought people to the Vashon ferry. The Matsudas rode the ferry to Seattle. Once there, they boarded a train with other Japanese American families. After three days, the train stopped near Fresno, California. The Matsudas and other families were forced into a temporary prison camp at the county fairgrounds. Later they were forced to get on a train that was headed to Tule Lake Relocation Center. This prison camp was on a dry lakebed in northeast California. A barbed-wire electric fence surrounded the camp. Guards watched over the prisoners from towers.

Mary and her family were imprisoned at Tule Lake for two years. By the time they were allowed to leave in 1944, more

PERSPECTIVES

WORLD WAR II

World War II broke out after Germany invaded Poland in 1939. Japan and Italy fought alongside Germany. These countries called themselves the Axis powers. They opposed the Allied powers. The Allied countries included Britain, France, China, and the Soviet Union. The United States had not wanted to get involved in the war. But tensions between the United States and Japan had been increasing. Japan wanted to control the South Pacific. So Japanese forces decided to attack Pearl Harbor.

PRISON CAMP LOCATIONS

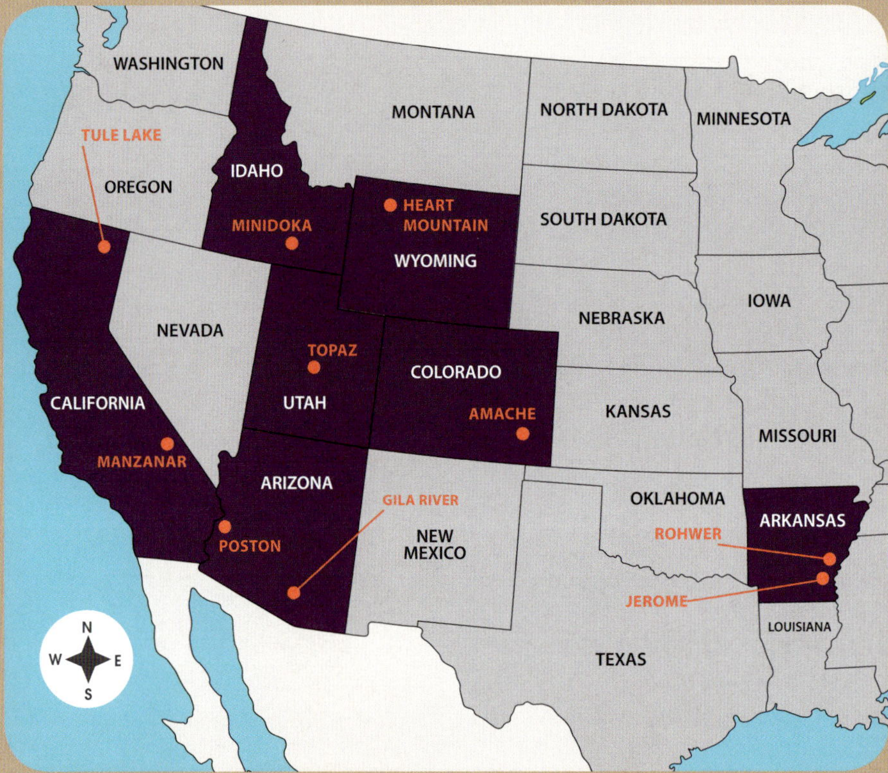

This map shows some of the largest camps where Japanese Americans were imprisoned during World War II. In what parts of the country were most camps located? Why do you think the US government chose to build camps in these areas?

than 18,000 Japanese Americans were imprisoned at the camp.

IMPRISONMENT

Nearly 120,000 Japanese Americans were forced into prison camps during World War II. Most lived on the

West Coast of the United States. Some Americans suspected that Japanese Americans on the West Coast might help the Japanese. So President Franklin D. Roosevelt decided all Japanese Americans needed to be moved away from the coast. US soldiers forced Japanese Americans into prison camps. This period of imprisonment would affect generations of Japanese Americans.

MARY MATSUDA GRUENEWALD

Mary Matsuda finished high school while she was in the Tule Lake prison camp. Volunteer teachers educated her and other Japanese Americans. After the war ended, she became a nurse. She married a man named Charles Gruenewald. She changed her name to Mary Matsuda Gruenewald. She worked as a nurse for more than 25 years. When she was 80 years old, Matsuda Gruenewald's book *Looking Like the Enemy* was published. In the book, she described her experiences at Tule Lake. In June 2017, Vashon Island High School invited her to its graduation ceremony. She walked in the ceremony. She was 92 years old. The school gave her a diploma.

CHAPTER TWO

IMMIGRATION

Prejudice against Asian Americans was widespread in the United States long before World War II. In the mid-1800s, thousands of Chinese people came to the United States. Gold had been discovered in California in 1848. Many Chinese immigrants became gold miners. They hoped to find wealth and better opportunities in the United States.

Many white settlers saw Chinese workers as their competitors. They disliked Chinese people simply because they looked different and spoke another language. They pressured the US Congress to pass a law in 1882. The law was commonly called the

Many white Americans tried to push Japanese Americans out of their communities in the early 1900s.

Chinese Exclusion Act. It banned Chinese laborers from entering the country.

Around the same time, Japanese immigrants started to come to the United States. For approximately 250 years, the Japanese government had not allowed people in Japan to immigrate to the United States. Then in 1853, the countries began trading goods with each other. This later led to the end of restrictions on immigration to the United States.

Between 1886 and 1911, more than 400,000 people left Japan for the United States. They were looking for work and ways to make better lives for themselves. Most settled in Hawaii or on the Pacific Coast. Approximately half of them became farmers. Others worked for or started businesses. Many Americans who resented Chinese immigrants also disliked Japanese immigrants. Japanese American farmers grew fruits and vegetables on land that white settlers had not been able to farm. White farmers did not like the fact that

In the early 1900s, many Japanese Americans settled in a part of San Francisco, California, that is known today as Japantown.

Japanese American farmers were more successful than them. They saw Japanese American farmers as a threat.

LAWS AND RESTRICTIONS

In the early 1900s, many white Americans tried to restrict the rights of Asian Americans. Labor leaders in

In the early 1900s, many Asian immigrants were processed at Angel Island Immigration Station in San Francisco, California.

San Francisco, California, formed the Asiatic Exclusion League in 1905. This group's mission was to ban Asian immigrants from coming to the United States. Then in 1906, the San Francisco school board tried to ban Asian Americans from public schools. The school board wanted to send them to separate schools.

Japanese Americans only made up a small part of the US population. Still, racist groups tried to exclude them from their communities. Some newspapers published stories that depicted Japanese people as enemies. Then in 1908, the US and Japanese governments made a deal called the Gentlemen's Agreement. Japan agreed to limit immigration to the United States. The United States would only allow entry to wives, children, and other relatives of immigrants already in the country.

In 1913 California lawmakers passed the Alien Land Law. This law prevented noncitizens from owning land. Japanese immigrants were not allowed to become citizens at the time. To get around this

PERSPECTIVES

CONFLICT

In 1904 war broke out between Russia and Japan. This conflict was called the Russo-Japanese War. Both countries wanted control of Korea and Manchuria. Manchuria was a region in northeastern China. Japan won the war in 1905. This made Japan the first Asian nation to defeat a European nation in modern times. For some Americans, this was another reason to see Japanese people as a threat.

GENERATIONS

Japanese Americans use different names to distinguish first-generation immigrants from second-generation immigrants. Immigrants born in Japan are called issei. *Issei* means "first generation" in Japanese. The issei call their children who were born in the United States nisei. *Nisei* means "second generation" in Japanese. In the early 1900s, issei often spoke only Japanese. Many ate traditional foods and followed Japanese customs. The nisei spoke English. They were more drawn to US cultures and customs.

law, some Japanese Americans used European names when they registered their property. Others used the names of their children who had been born in the United States. Since they had been born in the country, they were citizens.

In 1924 the Immigration Act passed. It was commonly called the Johnson-Reed Act. This law banned all Asian immigrants from entering the United States.

STRAIGHT TO THE SOURCE

Theodore Roosevelt was the US president in the early 1900s. On December 3, 1906, he gave a speech before Congress. He spoke about the growing anti-Japanese attitude among Americans. He said,

> *The overwhelming mass of our people cherish a lively regard and respect for the people of Japan. . . . But here and there a most unworthy feeling has manifested itself toward the Japanese—the feeling that has been shown in shutting them out from the common schools in San Francisco, and in mutterings against them in one or two other places, because of their efficiency as workers. . . . We have as much to learn from Japan as Japan has to learn from us; and no nation is fit to teach unless it is also willing to learn.*

Source: Theodore Roosevelt. "State of the Union Address Part II (1906)." *Teaching American History*. Ashbrook Center, 2019. Web. Accessed June 10, 2019.

What's the Big Idea?

Take a close look at this passage. What point was Roosevelt trying to make? How did he describe the relationships between white Americans and the Japanese?

CHAPTER THREE

PEARL HARBOR

In the 1930s, the United States' relationship with Japan became strained. Japan invaded China in 1937. War broke out between Japan and China. President Franklin D. Roosevelt opposed the invasion. He did not allow war supplies to be sent to Japan. Japanese forces were aggressive. They attacked Chinese people. In response, US officials restricted trade with Japan even further. They hoped the Japanese army would not have enough supplies to keep fighting. As a result of this political tension, many Americans began to distrust Japanese people even more.

Japanese Americans attend church in Oakland, California, in the early 1940s.

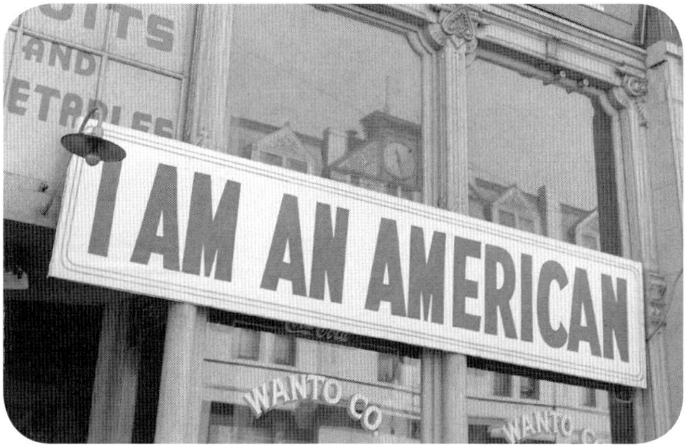

After the Pearl Harbor attack, some Japanese Americans created signs that read "I Am an American" to show people they were loyal to the United States.

In 1940 Japanese officials signed a pact with Germany and Italy. They joined the Axis powers. Then US officials cut off all trade with Japan.

Japanese forces soon planned an attack on the United States. US officials did not think the Japanese would attack Pearl Harbor. The naval base was in the middle of the Pacific Ocean. It was approximately 2,000 miles (3,000 km) from the US mainland and 4,000 miles (6,000 km) from Japan. So when Japanese forces bombed Pearl Harbor on December 7, 1941, the US military was unprepared.

The Pearl Harbor attack killed 2,403 Americans. Another 1,178 were injured. The day after the attack,

Roosevelt declared war on Japan. The United States entered World War II.

PANIC SPREADS

In 1941 approximately 113,000 Japanese Americans lived in California, Washington, and Oregon. Two-thirds of them were US citizens. The Federal Bureau of Investigation (FBI) arrested approximately 3,000 Japanese American community and religious leaders. There was no evidence that they had broken any law. But the US government froze their bank accounts. They could not withdraw any money.

PERSPECTIVES

GEORGE TAKEI

George Takei is a Japanese American actor. In the 1940s, Takei and his family were forced from their home at gunpoint. They were put in a camp in Arkansas. Takei did not understand how he could be both a US citizen and a prisoner. He said, "I was five years old at the beginning of our internment in Arkansas. I remember every school morning reciting the Pledge of Allegiance, my eyes upon the stars and stripes of the [US] flag, but at the same time I could see from the window the barbed wire and the sentry towers where guards kept guns trained on us."

In February 1941, Roosevelt asked John Franklin Carter to find out whether Japanese Americans on the West Coast were a threat. Carter was the director of the White House intelligence team. This team collected information to protect the United States from threats. Carter assured the president that the Japanese Americans were loyal to the United States. But other people thought Japanese Americans were threats.

JAPANESE AMERICANS IN HAWAII

Approximately 150,000 Japanese Americans lived in Hawaii before the Pearl Harbor attack. After the attack, political leaders called for the arrest of Japanese Americans in Hawaii. But wealthy landowners opposed this plan. One-third of all Hawaiians were of Japanese descent. Without them, there would not have been enough workers to grow food and run shops on the Hawaiian Islands. So the US military did not remove all Japanese Americans in Hawaii. Fewer than 1,500 Japanese Americans from Hawaii were sent to prison camps on the mainland.

In January 1942, the FBI forced some of the Japanese Americans it had arrested into prison camps. These camps were in Montana, New Mexico, and North Dakota.

On February 19, 1942, Roosevelt signed Executive Order 9066. This order gave the secretary of war the power to remove people from certain areas. Henry Stimson was the secretary of war at the time. He quickly removed all Japanese Americans from the West Coast. The US military moved them into prison camps.

FURTHER EVIDENCE

Chapter Three describes the Pearl Harbor attack and its aftermath. What was one of the main points of this chapter? What evidence is included to support this point? Read the article at the website below. Does the information on the website support the point you identified? Or does it offer a new piece of evidence?

CIVIL RIGHTS: JAPANESE AMERICANS

abdocorelibrary.com/japanese-american-imprisonment

CHAPTER
FOUR

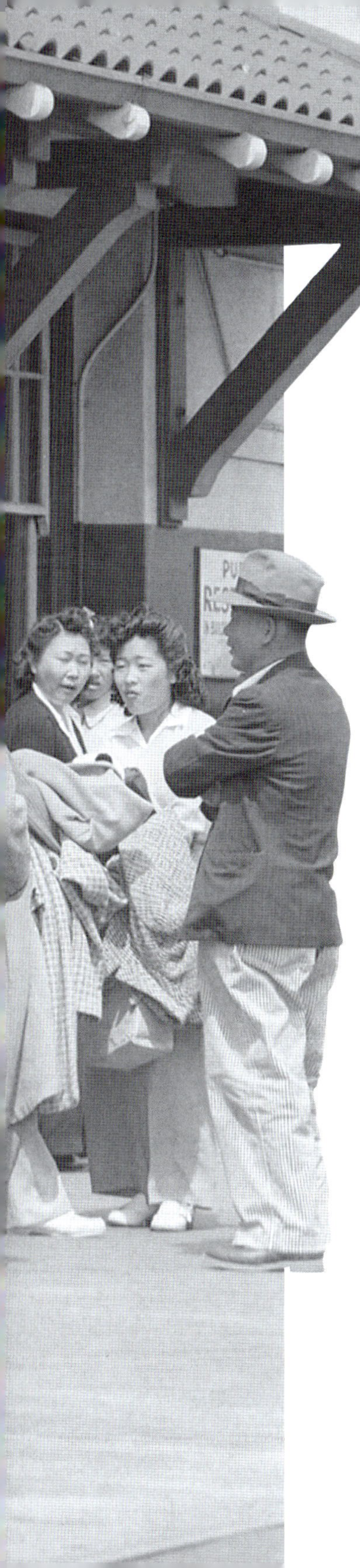

LIFE IN PRISON

In March 1942, the US military posted signs in California, Oregon, Washington, and Arizona. All Japanese Americans were to report to nearby centers. They had between four days and two weeks to arrive. They could bring only what they could carry. They did not have time to sell their land, homes, or businesses for a fair price. They had to take what they could get.

The prison camps were not yet ready. Japanese Americans were held in temporary assembly centers while the camps were prepared. They had to stay in animal stables or barns. The largest center was the Santa Anita

Japanese Americans in San Pedro, California, wait for a train that will relocate them to a prison camp in 1942.

Racetrack near downtown Los Angeles, California. Military police held more than 18,000 people in horse stalls there. Barbed-wire fences surrounded the assembly centers. Most Japanese Americans were held in the centers for three months.

PERSPECTIVES

SUPREME COURT RULINGS

Four Japanese Americans were jailed when they refused to go to prison camps. They each took their cases to the US Supreme Court. They argued that the US Constitution guaranteed them civil rights as US citizens. The government was not allowed to treat them differently based on their race. The Supreme Court ruled that their removal was not based on racism. The court said it was a wartime necessity.

FOOD AND HOUSING

By the fall of 1942, the US government had opened many prison camps. The government called them "relocation centers." The government did not consider them to be prison camps. But the people in these camps usually could not leave. Armed guards

PRISON CAMP POPULATIONS

CAMP NAME	PEAK POPULATION
Tule Lake	18,789
Poston	17,814
Gila River	13,348
Heart Mountain	10,767
Manzanar	10,046
Minidoka	9,397
Jerome	8,497
Rohwer	8,475
Topaz	8,130
Amache	7,318

This chart shows the peak populations at ten of the largest prison camps. Which camps had the largest populations? Why do you think this was?

watched over them. For these reasons, the places were prison camps.

The prison camps were in remote places with harsh weather. Two were in California, and two were in Arizona. Another two were in Arkansas. Other camps were in Idaho, Utah, Colorado, and Wyoming. Each camp held approximately 7,000 to 18,000 people. Small buildings called barracks served as housing. Four or five families lived together in one barrack. The buildings did little to keep out dust, heat, and cold. Prisoners used stoves to warm themselves in the winter. They slept on cots. They shared bathrooms and laundry rooms. Hot water was in short supply. It was hard to get healthy food and stay clean. Illnesses spread quickly since many people lived in close quarters. Many prisoners got sick.

Families ate together in large cafeterias with long tables and benches. Each hall served 500 people in three shifts. Japanese Americans were used to eating steamed rice and fish. They grew their own fruits and vegetables. But in most camps, their diets were limited. They were given potatoes, hot dogs, ham, and bread. Government officials hoped the prisoners would grow their own food. But even experienced farmers could not grow food from the dry soil at some of the camps.

SCHOOL AND WORK

Young prisoners went to schools in the camps. The classrooms were crowded. There were up to

At the prison camp schools, there were often not enough books or school supplies for everyone.

48 students for each teacher. Classes were held in one of the barracks.

Despite the bleak conditions, camp prisoners found ways to entertain themselves. They formed sports teams. They played softball, baseball, and football. They did arts and crafts. They performed plays and musicals.

WARTIME WORK

Despite the poor soil, prisoners in some camps were able to raise animals and grow vegetables. By the end of 1943, the camps grew 85 percent of their own vegetables. Because many men were serving in the military during World War II, farms outside of the camps needed workers. In some cases, prisoners were allowed to work outside the camps. In 1942 some prisoners were temporarily released to work on sugar beet farms in the West. In Arkansas, workers from prison camps cleared thousands of acres and worked in sawmills.

They also held on to their traditions and beliefs, including their religious beliefs. They set up Christian and Buddhist places of worship in the camps.

Each camp had a hospital, store, school, and police and fire departments. Camps also published newspapers. Prisoners could get jobs in the camps. Some cleaned and cooked in the kitchens. Others worked as cashiers in the camp stores. People wrote, printed, and sold newspapers. Still others worked as teachers, nurses, doctors, or dentists. There was also a need for people to work on building projects for the camps. The prisoners were paid a small wage. This payment was not nearly as much as what they could make outside of the camps.

UNDER THREAT

Like the assembly centers, the prison camps were surrounded by barbed-wire fences. Military guards with guns stood watch at all times. Anyone who tried to leave the camps would be shot. For most prisoners, this stressful way of life lasted three years.

EXPLORE ONLINE

Chapter Four discusses what life was like for Japanese Americans in the prison camps. The article at the website below also describes life in the camps. How is the information from the website the same as the information in Chapter Four? What new information did you learn?

LIFE IN THE CAMPS
abdocorelibrary.com/japanese-american-imprisonment

CHAPTER FIVE

THE AFTERMATH

In December 1944, the US military announced it would close the Japanese American prison camps. The Allied countries had won many battles. The war would end soon. Many young men had been released from the camps to fight in the war. Other Japanese Americans had been allowed to leave the camps if they went to school or found jobs in the Midwest or East.

On May 7, 1945, Germany surrendered. World War II ended in Europe. But Japan still fought the United States. US officials decided to try to force Japan to surrender. They planned attacks on Japan.

Japanese Americans had to endure cold winters in the prison camps.

On August 6, 1945, a US bomber plane dropped an atomic bomb over the Japanese city of Hiroshima. The explosion killed 80,000 people. Tens of thousands later died from exposure to radiation. Another atomic bomb was dropped on Nagasaki, Japan, three days later. It killed 40,000 people. On August 15, Japan surrendered.

By March 1946, the last Japanese American prison camp had closed. Thousands of Japanese Americans were freed. But they faced many challenges. They had to find new places to live. Many were old, poor, and sick.

LIFE AFTER IMPRISONMENT

The Doi family was one of the first Japanese American families to return to California. They were not welcomed back into their home community. White men blew up the shed at the Doi family home. They shot bullets into the house. The men were arrested but found not guilty. Between January and June 1945, 30 similar

Japanese American World War II veterans visit a monument in Los Angeles that honors Japanese American soldiers.

attacks occurred as Japanese Americans returned to the West Coast.

Many Japanese Americans had no home to return to. Because they had not paid their taxes, the government had taken their homes. Japanese Americans also struggled to find jobs. Many employers would not hire them. Some towns posted signs saying Japanese Americans were not welcome. Many Japanese

The Manzanar National Historic Site shows what Japanese American prisoners' living areas looked like at the Manzanar camp.

Americans left the West Coast. They hoped to find new homes and more opportunities in other parts of the county.

APOLOGIES

As years passed after World War II, the US government eventually admitted it had unjustly treated Japanese Americans. In July 1946, President Harry Truman met with the 442nd Regimental Combat Team. This was a group of Japanese American soldiers. Truman praised them for being loyal Americans.

In 1976 President Gerald Ford repealed Executive Order 9066. He apologized for the mass imprisonment of Japanese Americans. He promised that such an act of injustice would not happen again.

In 1988 President Ronald Reagan signed the Civil Liberties Act into law. The US government officially apologized to Japanese Americans. It gave each living camp survivor $20,000. Many Japanese Americans did not think these actions were enough to make up for their mistreatment. Japanese Americans had lost many things, including years of freedom.

JAPANESE AMERICAN SOLDIERS

In 1943 the US military needed more soldiers to help fight in the war. More than 2,600 Japanese Americans from Hawaii and 1,500 from the mainland signed up to fight. They made up the 442nd Regimental Combat Team. This team became the most decorated unit in US military history for its size and length of service. The unit's motto was "Go for Broke." It meant that the soldiers were ready to take on any risk in order to win.

PERSPECTIVES

LEARNING FROM MISTAKES

At Mary Matsuda Gruenewald's graduation ceremony in 2017, a student said, "We can't be against a whole group just because they're an 'other,' and we can't judge a whole group of people based on the actions of a few. As a society, I don't think we learn—because we sweep unpleasant things we've done under the carpet. So we're ashamed of what we've done and we don't want to remember it. But the whole point of history is to know what we've done in the past, and what mistakes we've made—and not repeat them."

LEARNING FROM HISTORY

The US Constitution protects the rights of all US citizens. But the World War II US prison camps denied the rights of many Americans. Today, many Japanese Americans have come forward to tell their stories. They hope to remind Americans of the importance of freedom. They also hope that by learning this history, Americans will not repeat the mistakes of the past.

STRAIGHT TO THE SOURCE

Japanese American Fred Korematsu was arrested in 1942 for refusing to go to a prison camp. He brought his case to the US Supreme Court in 1944. The court ruled against him. Korematsu's conviction was finally overturned in 1983. Afterward, Korematsu made this statement:

> *I thought that this [Supreme Court] decision was wrong and I still feel that way. As long as my record stands in federal court, any American citizen can be held in prison or concentration camps without a trial or a hearing. That is if they look like the enemy of our country. Therefore, I would like to see the government admit that they were wrong and do something about it so this will never happen again to any American citizen of any race, creed or color.*

Source: "Fred T. Korematsu." *Fred T. Korematsu Institute.* Fred T. Korematsu Institute, n.d. Web. Accessed July 3, 2019.

Consider Your Audience

Adapt this passage for a different audience, such as a friend or sibling. Write a blog post conveying this same information for the new audience. How does your post differ from the original text and why?

FAST FACTS

- Many Japanese Americans immigrated to the United States in the late 1800s. White settlers saw Japanese Americans as competitors for jobs. They discriminated against Japanese Americans.
- Approximately 120,000 Japanese Americans lived on the West Coast of the United States at the start of World War II.
- Japan supported Germany and Italy in World War II. In response, the United States cut off all trade with Japan.
- Japan bombed Pearl Harbor, Hawaii, on December 7, 1941.
- The US Congress declared war on Japan on December 8, 1941.
- Roosevelt issued Executive Order 9066 on February 19, 1942. This order allowed the US military to remove people from certain areas.
- By the fall of 1942, the US government had opened many prison camps in remote parts of the country. Japanese American prisoners were held in these camps.
- The last prison camp closed in 1946. Many Japanese Americans did not have homes to return to after their release from the camps. They faced widespread discrimination.

- In 1976 President Gerald Ford repealed Executive Order 9066.
- In 1988 President Ronald Reagan signed the Civil Liberties Act. The act gave each living camp survivor $20,000.

STOP AND THINK

Surprise Me

Chapter Two discusses anti-Asian attitudes in the United States before World War II. After reading this book, what two or three facts about this time period did you find most surprising? Write a few sentences about each fact. Why did you find each fact surprising?

You Are There

Chapter Four describes life in a Japanese American prison camp during World War II. Imagine you were visiting one of these camps. Write a letter home telling your friends or family about the camp. What is daily life like in the camp? Be sure to add plenty of details to your letter.

Dig Deeper

After reading this book, what questions do you still have about Japanese American imprisonment during World War II? With an adult's help, find a few reliable sources that can help you answer your questions. Write a paragraph about what you learned.

GLOSSARY

atomic bomb
a type of powerful bomb that goes off when atoms split apart

barrack
a military-style building where soldiers normally live

civil rights
the basic human rights that all people should have

descent
the origin or background of a person's blood-related family

immigrant
a person who comes to a country to live there permanently

prejudice
a feeling of dislike toward a group of people based on their race or other characteristics

racism
the belief that one race is superior to all others

radiation
a dangerous type of energy that is given off by certain substances

remote
far away from other people or settlements

repeal
to officially overturn something such as a law

settler
someone who settles in a new region or colony, often with a group

ONLINE RESOURCES

To learn more about Japanese American imprisonment during World War II, visit our free resource websites below.

Core Library CONNECTION
FREE! COMMON CORE MULTIMEDIA RESOURCES

Visit **abdocorelibrary.com** or scan this QR code for free Common Core resources for teachers and students, including vetted activities, multimedia, and booklinks, for deeper subject comprehension.

Booklinks NONFICTION NETWORK
FREE! ONLINE NONFICTION RESOURCES

Visit **abdobooklinks.com** or scan this QR code for free additional online weblinks for further learning. These links are routinely monitored and updated to provide the most current information available.

LEARN MORE

Lanier, Wendy H. *Life during World War II.* Minneapolis, MN: Abdo Publishing, 2015.

Warren, Andrea. *Enemy Child.* New York: Holiday House, 2019.

ABOUT THE AUTHORS

Duchess Harris, JD, PhD

Dr. Harris is a professor of American Studies at Macalester College and curator of the Duchess Harris Collection of ABDO books. She is also the coauthor of the titles in the collection, which features popular selections such as *Hidden Human Computers: The Black Women of NASA* and series including News Literacy and Being Female in America.

Before working with ABDO, Dr. Harris authored several other books on the topics of race, culture, and American history. She served as an associate editor for *Litigation News*, the American Bar Association Section of Litigation's quarterly flagship publication, and was the first editor in chief of *Law Raza*, an interactive online journal covering race and the law, published at William Mitchell College of Law. She has earned a PhD in American Studies from the University of Minnesota and a JD from William Mitchell College of Law.

Marne Ventura

Marne Ventura has written more than 100 books for children. A former elementary teacher, she holds a master's degree in education from the University of California. Marne and her husband live on the central coast of California.

INDEX